The Marquis de Lafayette Collection
Peachtree City Library

In Loving Memory of M.R. and D.B. Wingo

Marquis de Lafayette
Soldier, Statesman, American Hero
1757-1834

"Humanity has won its battle.
Liberty now has a country."

Paul Revere's Ride

by Lucia Raatma

Content Adviser: David F. Wood,
Curator, Concord Museum,
Concord, Massachusetts

Reading Adviser: Dr. Linda D. Labbo,
Department of Reading Education, College of Education,
The University of Georgia

COMPASS POINT BOOKS

Minneapolis, Minnesota

Compass Point Books
3109 West 50th Street, #115
Minneapolis, MN 55410

Visit Compass Point Books on the Internet at *www.compasspointbooks.com*
or e-mail your request to *custserv@compasspointbooks.com*

Editors: E. Russell Primm, Emily J. Dolbear, Halley Gatenby, and Catherine Neitge
Photo Researcher: Svetlana Zhurkina
Photo Selector: Linda S. Koutris
Designer/Page Production: Bradfordesign, Inc./Biner Design
Cartographer: XNR Productions, Inc.

Library of Congress Cataloging-in-Publication Data
Raatma, Lucia.
   Paul Revere's ride / by Lucia Raatma.
      p. cm. — (We the people)
   Includes bibliographical references and index.
Summary: Profiles the life of Paul Revere, silversmith and patriot, best known for his ride through the Massachusetts countryside, warning that the British were coming.
   ISBN 0-7565-0492-9 (hardcover : alk. paper)
   1. Revere, Paul, 1735–1818—Juvenile literature. 2. Statesmen—Massachusetts—Biography—Juvenile literature. 3. Massachusetts—Biography—Juvenile literature. 4. Massachusetts—History—Revolution, 1775–1783—Juvenile literature. 5. Massachusetts—History—Revolution, 1775–1783. [1. Revere, Paul, 1735–1818. 2. Revolutionaries. 3. Silversmiths.] I. Title. II. Series: We the people (Compass Point Books)
   F69.R43R33 2003
   973.3'311'092—dc21   2002155833

TABLE OF CONTENTS

NOTE: *In this book, words that are defined in the glossary are in* **bold** *the first time they appear in the text.*

HERO FOR A NEW NATION

"Listen, my children, and you shall hear
Of the midnight ride of Paul Revere,
On the eighteenth of April, in Seventy-five,
Hardly a man is now alive
Who remembers that famous day and year."

This is the beginning of *Paul Revere's Ride,* a poem written in 1860 by Henry Wadsworth Longfellow. The poem was published in the *Atlantic Monthly* magazine in 1861—more than eighty years after Paul Revere made his famous ride. Few people knew anything about Revere before then. However, the poem turned him

Henry Wadsworth Longfellow wrote Paul Revere's Ride *in 1860.*

into a national hero. Some details of the ride were exaggerated in the poem, but Revere remains an important figure in U.S. history. He was a strong member of the community in Boston, Massachusetts, and his actions helped lead to the Revolutionary War (1775–1783). Revere's bravery played a major role in creating the new nation that became the United States of America.

Paul Revere, silversmith and proud American

A SILVERSMITH AND MORE

Paul Revere was born on December 21, 1734. He grew up in the north end of Boston, Massachusetts. During the 1700s, Boston was a busy and exciting place. It was one of

6

Paul Revere's house was built in Boston in 1681.

the most important cities in the American **colonies.** Other key colonial cities were Philadelphia and New York. Ships carrying goods from England often docked at Boston Harbor, and the city's streets were filled with merchants and craftspeople.

Paul's mother was Deborah Hichborn Revere of Boston. His father was Apollos Rivoire, a Frenchman who came to the American colonies and later changed his name to Paul Revere. The elder Revere made a living as a goldsmith and silversmith, and he taught these metal-working skills to young Paul.

This bookplate was engraved by Paul Revere's father during the 1720s.

Revere made items such as this engraved teapot in his silver shop.

In addition to serving as an **apprentice** to his father, Paul also attended the North Writing School. His parents had many children—possibly as many as twelve. Paul was the oldest surviving son in the family. He was only a teenager when his father died. At that time, he took over the silversmith shop and tried to support his family.

As a silversmith, young Revere made silver cups, teapots, pitchers, rings, candlesticks, spoons, and a wide variety of other items. He also earned money by ringing the bells at Christ Church, a place of worship that is now called Old North Church. The church bells told Boston's citizens of special events, such as holidays, emergencies, and important news.

When Revere was in his early twenties, the French and Indian War (1754–1763) began. French soldiers had joined Native Americans to attack some of the American colonies. Revere was quick to defend his home, so he

A battle during the French and Indian War

9

volunteered to fight for the colonies. As a second lieutenant in the colonial forces, he spent the summer of 1756 at
Lake George, New York. However, he saw no battles and
soon headed home to Boston.

The next year,
Revere married Sarah
Orne, and they
eventually had
eight children
together. In 1773,
Sarah died, and
Paul married
Rachel Walker.
They also had eight
children. Sadly,
many of the sixteen
Revere children died
when they were very young.

Rachel Walker was Revere's second wife,
and the mother of eight of his children.

Over the years, Revere hired many people to work in his silversmith shop. Young men served as apprentices and **journeymen.** Revere and his staff produced some of the finest silver pieces of the day. In addition, Revere worked as a copper-plate engraver. With this skill, he created **bookplates,** cartoons, and illustrations for magazines and other publications. He also worked as a dentist for several years, cleaning people's teeth and making dentures out of ivory or the teeth of animals. Between his responsibilities at work and at home, Revere had much to do. However, that did not stop him from taking on an important cause—helping the American colonies gain freedom from the British.

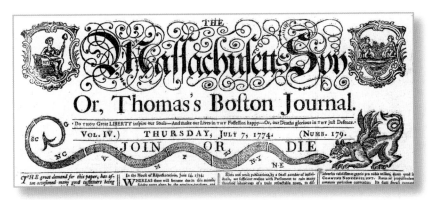

Revere engraved this top part of the July 1774 issue of the Massachusetts Spy Or, Thomas's Boston Journal.

SONS OF LIBERTY

The American colonies were controlled by Great Britain. However, many colonists did not like being ruled by King George III and the British **Parliament.** They believed the king's rules—especially his taxes—were unfair. Since the colonies had no voice in British government, they did not want to support that nation by paying taxes.

King George III of England imposed taxes that colonists thought were unfair.

A group of colonists met and discussed ways to stand up to Britain. These **Patriots** called themselves the Sons of Liberty. One night, the Sons of Liberty did something bold

A meeting of the Sons of Liberty to discuss ways to stand up to the British

13

Patriots disguised as Native Americans dumped tea from British ships into
Boston Harbor in December 1773.

and dangerous. On December 16, 1773, they dressed up as Native Americans by painting their faces and wearing blankets as clothing. Carrying axes, they next crept into Boston Harbor, where three shiploads of British tea were awaiting delivery. This tea had been sent from England to Boston, where the American colonists would have to pay taxes on it.

Under the cover of night, the Sons of Liberty leapt onto the ships. They found the large containers of tea and broke them open with their axes. These Patriots then dumped the tea into the harbor. Some say they destroyed 10,000 pounds (4,536 kilograms) of tea, worth tens of thousands of dollars.

This event came to be known as the Boston Tea Party, and it marked the beginning of the Patriots' revolution. After the tea had been dumped into the harbor, Paul Revere delivered the news to towns from Boston to New York to Philadelphia. He rode on horseback for several days, bringing the colonists word of the Patriots' actions.

British troops entering Boston to make sure the colonists obeyed the tax laws

King George III was angry about the Boston Tea

Party. Parliament passed a number of laws that made life

hard for the colonists. The colonists called these laws the

Intolerable Acts because they could not tolerate, or put up with, living under them. More and more, the colonists knew it was time to rule themselves.

For the next several months, Revere became the most important messenger between Boston and Philadelphia. Television and radio did not yet exist, of course, so having

Revere distributes notices containing important news as he rides through a village during the 1770s.

17

people deliver news on horseback was often the fastest way to spread information. Revere also began secretly working against the British. He spied on the soldiers and watched

Minutemen were Patriots who said they could be ready to fight the British in a minute.

18

their movements. It was Revere's job to tell the other Patriots about any plans the British were making.

This was a dangerous job for Revere. He had to watch the British without being seen by them. Sometimes he got caught and had to answer questions the British soldiers asked him. A few of these times, he was even locked up in prison. Fortunately, Revere always managed to come up with an excuse for his actions, and he continued to keep a watchful eye on the British soldiers.

As feelings between the American colonists and the British got worse, King George III sent more troops to the colonies. The colonists would not back down, though. Instead, they armed themselves and got ready for war. A group of Patriots called themselves minutemen. The name meant they could be ready to fight in a minute if they had to.

THE MIDNIGHT RIDE

By April 1775, British troops were searching the areas around Boston for war supplies that they believed the colonists had hidden. Like the Patriots, the British were also preparing for a conflict. British ships were in the harbor. Neither the British soldiers nor the colonists wanted to fight. On the other hand, neither side wanted

British warships in Boston Harbor during the 1770s

to back down, either. No one doubted that war was on the way.

On the evening of April 18, Paul Revere was asked to meet with Dr. Joseph Warren, a man who was heading all the Patriot actions in Boston. Warren told Revere to ride to Lexington, Massachusetts. Once he arrived, Revere was to find Patriot leaders Samuel Adams and John Hancock. Adams had spoken out

Dr. Joseph Warren was the leader of the Patriots in Boston.

against the British for some time, and he had planned the Boston Tea Party. Hancock was a rich businessman who had been working for the colonists' freedom. Warren told

John Hancock led the colonists in their fight for freedom.

Revere to warn the two men that the British troops were coming. If the British caught them, Adams and Hancock would be arrested for working against the king.

Revere had already known for a few days that this important ride was going to happen soon. He had arranged a special signal with someone at Christ Church. One lantern would be hung in the church if the British were moving by land. That meant that the troops would be marching out Boston Neck, which was the only land route out of the city. Two lanterns would be hung if they were moving by sea. If that was the case, the

Paul Revere looks back at the bell tower of Christ Church.

colonists knew that the British would be crossing Boston's

Charles River to Cambridge, Massachusetts.

During their meeting on April 18, Warren informed

Revere that the troops were moving across the Charles River.

Revere went quickly to Christ Church and gave instructions for the two-lantern signal. Then he ran down to the Charles River, where two friends waited to row him to Charlestown. As they crossed the river, they drew dangerously close to the British ship *Somerset,* which was anchored nearby. They hoped that no one on board the ship would hear them. They even tied a cloth—some say a woman's petticoat—around their oars so they would make less noise in the water. Once in Charlestown, Revere borrowed a horse from a local church deacon. Then he set out on the midnight ride that Longfellow wrote about in his famous poem.

With the Charles River on one side and the Mystic River on the other, Revere rode through Charlestown and then headed toward Medford. After crossing a marshland called Charlestown Common, he came upon two British soldiers. No doubt his heart sank at the sight of them. One soldier tried to block his path, and the other soldier

24

got stuck in the mud. Revere managed to get around the men and sped into the night. He rode through the dark countryside that was lit only by a bright moon.

Revere avoided British soldiers on his moonlit ride to Lexington.

Revere rode through Massachusetts, warning townspeople and minutemen
that the British were coming.

Going from house to house and from town to town, Revere warned everyone he met that the British troops, or regulars, were coming. Minutemen quickly pulled on their boots and coats and began riding toward Concord, Massachusetts. They had stored guns and other supplies there, hoping to be ready for the British. They needed to reach those supplies before the British discovered them.

As Revere shouted his message during that midnight ride, he woke people—and perhaps he frightened them, too. The British had more men, horses, and guns than the Patriots. The colonists knew this, and most of them did not want to go to war. However, they did want to be free from British rule. Keeping this in mind, they tried to be brave as they left their homes and headed out into the night.

Once in Lexington, Revere woke up Adams and Hancock and warned them that the British troops were

27

on their way. The two men quickly prepared to leave town. Revere next met with William Dawes, another rider who had been sent from Boston. Dawes carried the same message as Revere, but he had traveled a different route. The two men decided to ride to Concord and planned to meet other Patriots where the supplies were stored. Soon they were joined by Samuel Prescott,

William Dawes also rode from Boston to Lexington on April 18, 1775. Like Revere, he helped warn the colonists about the British.

a young doctor returning to Concord after a visit with his fiancée. After meeting Revere along the way, Prescott became another rider who alerted colonists about the British.

Before they could reach Concord, however, the three men found themselves surrounded by British troops. Prescott and his horse quickly jumped a low wall and got away, and he continued his ride to Concord. Soon after, Dawes also managed to escape, leaving Revere to be questioned by the soldiers. They asked him his name and what he was doing out in the middle of the night. No doubt he was scared, but he tried not to show it. He boasted that he had left Boston at around ten o'clock and had been waking up the countryside, telling everyone about the British plans. The soldiers weren't sure what to believe, but they didn't take Revere seriously. They eventually released him, but they kept his horse.

LEXINGTON AND CONCORD

By the time the British soldiers released Paul Revere, it was well after midnight. Revere was exhausted. Without a horse, however, he had no choice but to walk. He decided to stay off the road, where more British troops might be marching, and instead hiked through the countryside. Through graveyards and pastures, over walls and streams, Revere traveled back to Lexington. There he found Adams and Hancock just getting into a carriage to leave. Revere rode along with them until he was sure they were safe. Then he walked back to Lexington again. While he was resting there, John Lowell, a man who worked for Hancock, came to Revere and asked for his help moving a trunk of important papers that Hancock had left behind.

The trunk John Hancock left behind in Lexington

As the sun was rising, Revere and Lowell reached the tavern where the papers had been left and found the trunk. By that time, Minutemen and other colonists had

The thirteen American colonies

gathered on Lexington Green and were waiting to surprise the British troops. Revere and Lowell quickly carried the trunk out of the tavern and across the green. They kept walking even as the British arrived and shots were fired! The two men managed to get Hancock's trunk to a safe place. Though the battle at Lexington was a short one, it marked the first gunfire of the Revolutionary War and the beginning of the colonists' fight for freedom.

The Battle of Lexington marked the beginning of the Revolutionay War.

After the battle at Lexington, the British troops moved on to Concord. There, they tried to locate the Patriots' supplies, but they were unsuccessful. When the British began a bonfire in the center of Concord, the Patriots feared they would burn down the whole town. To prevent

Minutemen chased British soldiers off North Bridge during the Battle of Concord.

this from happening, the Patriots entered Concord, and fighting broke out once again. There was a brief exchange of shots at North Bridge, and the British soldiers **retreated.**

The British troops marched back to Boston later that day, but the fighting was not over yet. Hundreds of Patriots hid in the woods along the road the British traveled. They shot at the British when they least expected it, and then they hid again. The Patriots had learned this style of battle from the Native Americans. The British troops had never been attacked this way before. They were used to more direct forms of fighting and were unsure how to deal with the Patriots.

By the time the British troops reached Boston, they were tired and had lost many men. The courage of the Patriots had surprised the British. They had new respect for the colonists. The Patriots' success that day would never have been possible without Paul Revere's famous ride.

AFTER THE RIDE

Paul Revere remained busy during the Revolutionary War. He continued to work as a messenger for the American cause, and he also served as a lieutenant colonel in the Massachusetts **militia.** Revere was disappointed that he never served in the Continental army, which was the main group of troops fighting the British. In fact, his military career was rather ordinary.

Members of the Continental army

In 1776, the Declaration of Independence was signed. This document officially told Great Britain that the American colonies were free from British rule. The fighting finally stopped in 1781. Two years later, the Americans signed a peace **treaty** with the British. The United States of America had become a new nation. By that time, Revere was in his late forties and had returned to his silversmith shop. He also ran a hardware store and opened a **foundry,** where he made cannons, bolts, nails, and bells. One of his bells still rings in Kings Chapel in Boston.

In addition, Revere opened the first North American mill to roll copper. This mill provided sheets of copper for ships, as well as for the dome on top of the Massachusetts

These nails and spikes were made at Revere's copper mill.

State House. Revere also created a line of pots and pans with copper bases. This cookware led to the creation of the Revereware brand of pots and pans, which is today produced by a different company.

The dome on top of the Massachusetts State House in Boston is made of copper from Revere's mill.

37

Paul Revere remained active in the community late into his life.

Well into his seventies, Revere remained busy in the Boston community. When he finally retired, he left his businesses to his sons and grandsons. In 1813, both Revere's wife, Rachel, and his son, Paul, died. This was a difficult time for him. Five years later, on May 10, 1818, Revere died from natural causes. The *Boston Intelligence* newspaper wrote, "Seldom has the tomb closed upon a life so honorable and useful."

Paul Revere's grave is located in the Granary Burying Ground in Boston.

40

A statue of Paul Revere in Boston

Paul Revere was not famous during his lifetime, and he was not a war hero. However, he provided important services and businesses to colonial Boston. Revere was a leader in his community and served the Patriot cause proudly. He showed bravery and determination in his activities as a messenger, and he assisted the colonies as they prepared for war with Britain.

His midnight ride in April 1775 called the minutemen to action and helped launch the Revolutionary War. Revere's courage is an example of the American spirit that still survives in the twenty-first century.

GLOSSARY

apprentice—a person who works for and learns from a skilled tradesperson for a certain amount of time

bookplates—labels that are placed in the front of books that list the owner's name

colonies—lands settled by people from another country and ruled by that country

foundry—a factory for melting and shaping metal

journeymen—people who have worked as an apprentice and learned a trade

militia—military force, often made up of local volunteers

Parliament—the part of the British government that makes laws

Patriots—American colonists who wanted their independence from Britain

treaty—an agreement between two governments

DID YOU KNOW?

- William Dawes, one of the riders in April 1775, was a talented actor. When he was occasionally stopped by British troops, he would pretend to be drunk so they would leave him alone.

- Some sources say that the horse Paul Revere rode was named Scheherazade. Others say it was Brown Beauty. Whatever the horse's name may have been, the British took it from Revere just outside of Concord.

- Revere died at the age of eighty-three. He was survived by five children, as well as many grandchildren and great-grandchildren. He was buried in the Granary Burying Ground in Boston.

- Seventy-five of the bells that Revere produced still ring throughout New England.

IMPORTANT DATES

Timeline

1734	Paul Revere is born in Boston, Massachusetts.
1756	Revere serves in the colonial forces during the French and Indian War.
1757	Revere marries Sarah Orne.
1773	Sarah Revere dies; Paul Revere marries Rachel Walker; in December, Revere delivers news of the Boston Tea Party.
1775	On April 18, Revere makes his famous ride to warn people of the British troops' advance; the next day, the Battles of Lexington and Concord take place.
1776	On July 4, the Declaration of Independence is signed.
1781	Revolutionary War fighting ends.
1783	Great Britain and the United States sign the Treaty of Paris.
1818	Paul Revere dies on May 10.
1860	Henry Wadsworth Longfellow writes the poem *Paul Revere's Ride;* it appears in the *Atlantic Monthly* the following year.

IMPORTANT PEOPLE

SAMUEL ADAMS
(1722–1803), *Patriot who led opposition to British rule of the colonies*

WILLIAM DAWES
(1745–1799), *Patriot messenger who accompanied Revere on part of his famous ride*

JOHN HANCOCK
(1737–1793), *leader of the Patriot cause; was the first person to sign the Declaration of Independence*

SAMUEL PRESCOTT
(1751–1777?), *doctor and Patriot who accompanied Paul Revere for part of his ride*

JOSEPH WARREN
(1741–1775), *doctor and leader of Patriot activities in Boston*

WANT TO KNOW MORE?

At the Library

Dell, Pamela A. *Freedom's Light: A Story About Paul Revere's Midnight Ride.*
Excelsior, Minn.: Tradition Books, 2002.

Grote, Joann A. *Paul Revere: American Patriot.* Broomall, Pa.: Chelsea
House, 1999.

Kallen, Stuart A. *Samuel Adams.* Edina, Minn.: Abdo & Daughters, 2002.

Kent, Deborah. *Lexington and Concord.* Danbury, Conn.: Children's
Press, 1998.

Sakurai, Gail. *Paul Revere.* Danbury, Conn.: Children's Press, 1997.

Sullivan, George. *Paul Revere.* New York: Scholastic Reference, 1999.

On the Web

For more information on *Paul Revere,* use FactHound

to track down Web sites related to this book.

1. Go to *www.facthound.com*

2. Type in a search word related to this book
   or this book ID: 0756504929.

3. Click on the *Fetch It* button.

Your trusty FactHound will fetch the best Web sites for you!

Through the Mail

Concord Museum

200 Lexington Road

Concord, MA 01742

For information on this historic town and the famous Revolutionary War

battle that occurred there

On the Road

Minute Man National Historical Park

174 Liberty Street

Concord, MA 01742

978/369-6993

To see where the Battle of Concord took place

The Paul Revere House

19 North Square

Boston, MA 02113

617/523-2338

To visit Revere's home

INDEX

About the Author

Lucia Raatma received her bachelor's degree in English literature from the University of South Carolina and her master's degree in cinema studies from New York University. She has written a wide range of books for young people. When she is not researching or writing, she enjoys going to movies, playing tennis, practicing yoga, and spending time with her husband, daughter, and golden retriever. She lives in New York.